M000265966

SOMEDANCE

SOMEDANCE
TIFFANY TWIST

et al.

Andover, MN

SOME DANCE © copyright 2005 by Tiffany Twist
All rights reserved. No part of this book may be reproduced in
any form whatsoever, by photography or xerography or by any
other means, by broadcast or transmission, by translation into any
kind of language, nor by recording electronically or otherwise, without permission in writing from the author, except by a reviewer,
who may quote brief passages in critical articles or reviews.

ISBN 13: 978-1-931945-30-1
ISBN 10: 1-931945-30-6

Library of Congress Catalog Number: 2005925588

Printed in the United States of America

First Printing: April 2005

09 08 07 06 05   5 4 3 2 1

et al. Publishing
An imprint of Expert Publishing, Inc.
14314 Thrush Street NW,
Andover, MN 55304-3330
1-877-755-4966
www.expertpublishinginc.com

PROLOGUE

What are you doing here?
Here, in my heart?
Who let you in?
Who invited you?
Did I somehow open the door?

Why is my heart crying out to you,
When my only reaction should be to run?
Run as fast as I can from the danger you hold,
From the destruction you could cause.
Why am I not strong enough to stay away?

My arms are weak.
I cannot stand.
My eyes demand to be shut.
My head is filled with thoughts of you,
To be with you, next to you, holding your hand.

Yet I am repulsed
At the sense of helplessness you bring,
As if a drug were secretly,
Unsuspectingly,
Slipped into my drink.

I hadn't asked.
I hadn't desired.
Yet you, somehow you,
Were placed into my drink,
My life.

I was not looking,
I was not guarding.
I turned my head,
And you were allowed
To be secretly placed into my heart.

And slowly,
You, the drug,
Released yourself into my system.
You flow through my veins,
Travel every inner inch of me.

Until you took over,
And thoughts of you ruled my being,
Ruled my days, my nights, even my sleep.
I cannot close my eyes,
And have a single thought apart from you.

I am one with the drug that flows through my body,
It has taken over,
And I can't stop its effect.
I've swallowed it, I've swallowed you,
And now you control my decisions, my actions.

When my body reacts,
It reacts to the feeling you have produced.
I do things that I would not have done
Had I been sober,
Apart from you.

How many have fallen to your seducing ways?
How many stories have I heard?
The acid told me to jump, jump out the window.
And there a body discovered,
Smashed upon the pavement.

Will you, too, tell me to jump?
Have you told me to jump?
You must have,
For right now I lie upon the pavement,
Paralyzed and unable to rise.

You have sickened me with love.
Why must this love make me feel so weak?
I am not myself and you have done it.
If I remain this way,
I will waste my life.

And you? What will you do with all of this?
If I want to be in your arms,
Will you keep me there?
Will you love me like no one else has loved me?
Will you keep me safe? Protect me?

Will you look into my eyes every day of my life?
Will you hold my face to yours?
And want nothing but to be by my side?
Or will you one day forget about me, too.
Like the one who shouldn't have.

Is there really such a thing?
As a love that is not forgotten?
A love that endures?
Or is it all a fairy tale?
An illusion?

I imagine nothing but to be next to you.
Hazy, weak, while next to you.
Shutting out the world and everything it contains.
Absent from thought that doesn't contain you.
Thoughts of the past, thoughts of the future.

Who are you and how did you do this to me?
Could you be everything I have waited for?
Everything I have longed for?
The one I have spent a lifetime searching for?
The one who has inhabited my dream state? Was it you?

Were those your eyes I hazily gazed into?
Was it your hand I held? Your lips I kissed?
Your waist I wrapped my arms around?
Your chest upon which I rested my head?
The one I dreaded being wakened and taken from?

And if it is so,
How can I stay away?
How do I forget?
Forget how you make me feel?
Forget your face? Forget your voice?

How can I ever walk away from you?
Put my back to you?
Then never turn around,
And in panic,
Run to catch you?

I have fallen in love with a man,
One from whom I should have fled.
He caught me unsuspecting.
I wasn't watching and he pulled me from my rooted land.
He took over my soul, and I need him.

Every cell encased in my body calls out to him.
Every inch of my being cries for him.
I have fallen in love with a man,
One from whom I should flee,
But can't.

The mass of men lead lives of quiet desperation.
—Henry David Thoreau

~~~~~~~~~~~~~~~~~

ONE

~~~~~~~~~

I wave a pair of scissors at him, the despised morning sun echoes off the hard metal of its blades, firing a screaming beam of light into his eyes.

"I'm going to cut it up."

My husband lifts his arm to block the piercing light stream that was most likely traveling straight through his liquid brain.

"I'm going to cut it to pieces."

I began to storm around the house.

Who was this man I was married to? Sitting like a zombie on the couch, slurring, cursing, unable to move, unwilling to make eye contact. And that look on his face, as if I'm looking at a contorted product of the devil himself.

I went toward the storage. I was going to find it, pull it out, and take these scissors to it. Instant divorce. Maybe not a real divorce, but it had to stand for something. I played it out in my mind, the stupid thing cut to shreds. Sparkling sequins falling to the floor, to their death. How could I have been so blind to believe in the happy ending?

I sat before the blue plastic tub and removed its cover. I cast my eyes toward the puffy white chiffon dress folded inside and glared at it with contempt as I tore it from its four-year resting place. Tears began to wet the material as my head became overwhelmed with thoughts of the events from only hours before.

It was the night of my sister's wedding, a celebration of two people pledging their lives to each other. To love, to have, to hold, forever. Then the celebration. Celebration—crap.

He and I had done it four years earlier, pledged ourselves into marital bliss. And then he threatened to leave me, blackmailed me with mass humiliation on my own wedding day. My husband of a whole six hours was ready to walk away from the one to whom he just pledged his love.

I waited for him, pacing the bright white hallway off the room filled with our wedding guests. I lifted my long white gown from its job as a dust mop for the hard vinyl floor. "Where are they?" I asked. Dinner was done, plates were cleared, and the deejay waited to start the music, but we had no groom, no bridesmaids. I sadly said good bye to many of the guests tired of waiting. I shrugged at others' inquiry about where they were or when we were going to start.

Finally, the female side of my wedding party and my new husband enter; he's laughing, his bow tie gone, shirt open. He loosened up after a few drinks with my attendants. Fine, but no time to chit chat, we need to get this party going.

It was our dance, our first dance as husband and wife. We're alone now on the dance floor. I ask him, "What were you thinking? Did you forget about me, did you forget we had a wedding here?" No apology. I push, "People left, sweetheart. What were you thinking?" We have smiles for the onlookers as we rock back and forth to the slow beat. He gets close to my ear and speaks slowly. "Say one more word and I walk off this floor." I stopped breathing for a moment as the vision filled my head. I would be left standing on this floor alone? Oh God, the music playing, everyone watching as he drops his arms from around my waist and turns his back on me, and walks away? I panicked, let out a little laugh to hide my horror from my audience, and didn't utter another word. I was stupid to think the whole wedding thing was going to stand for the happy ending I thought it should.

And so, four years later, on this celebration day with my sister and her new husband, we set out to whoop it up, friends, family, some drinking, some dancing.

Except for me. I was forced to stay sober, clear minded. I was pregnant with our second child. One could hardly tell at this point; I just seemed a little fat. Pregnancy seemed to hit my face and legs and bottom before my belly. Regardless, no drinks for me beyond some juice or soda, and, unfortunately, sobriety was not a wishful state for the scene I was about to behold.

The bridal party, about eight of us, filled the limo and we made a quick stop at a little place across town, for which I was grateful. I really had to visit the little girls' room. We jumped from the limo and headed for the door. The musty smell of liquor surrounded me the minute I stepped inside the bar, and pregnancy only made my senses keener. This place was going to make me nauseous, but not as nauseous as the little blonde and the man married to me would make me later.

Some of our group of eight went straight for shots, some to the bathroom, and I've established I was amongst the latter.

I emptied my pressed-upon bladder, washed my hands, and carefully placed my damp paper towel around the handle of the door to avoid catching that nasty stuff non-hand washers leave to spread to the unsuspecting world.

I exited the bathroom. I looked for my husband, half of me expecting him to be waiting outside the door for the woman he married, the mother of his son, the one carrying his second child. The other half of me, and most likely the more prominent half, expected him to be at the bar, downing a couple of drinks.

He was not occupying either of those spaces. I caught the back of him as he was heading toward the exit—with someone else, a blonde someone else.

He rested his hand lightly upon the small of her back; well, more like her tiny butt, oh, so sweetly escorting her toward the exit.

Escorting *her*!

I stood there. I thought, *he couldn't be that drunk that he thinks this five foot petite blonde is his wife, could he?*

Of course not, the jerk. I was five feet six and brunette. He *was* drunk, or at least on his way.

But is that an alibi? It's *his* alibi. Always is. And this wouldn't be the first, or last, time he would call upon his useful excuse.

We're barhopping, so the limo takes us to the next bar.

And here he's sitting on the stool next to *her*. Laughing, having the time of his life. Same little blonde. It's always a little blonde. If that's what he wanted, then why the hell did he marry me?

And he has no idea what he is doing. Not a clue. Smiling, leaning in close to her. And does he see her? Does he see the smile on her face as she looks over at me knowing full well it is my husband giving her the attention that was rightfully mine? I think at this point the man I married doesn't even remember he has a pregnant wife. Fine, as long as I'm not around to see it.

But flaunt it right in my face?

My un-intoxicated, fat, insecure face?

TWO

~~~~~~~~~~~~

I give him his sober cab home—again. Fat, extremely self-conscious, sober cabbie. That is me. I park my car in the driveway, glance over, and notice that his eyes were rolled into the back of his head.

I want to scratch them out.

I take my moment of opportunity and bolt out of the car, run into the house, and lock the door. I fly to the top of the stairs and go into a rage—a rage on myself.

I do that. Bring more torture on myself when I am in torture. I imagine torturing my torturer, then, in reality, turn the rage onto myself. I want to rip the hair from my head, every single strand.

Some time passes and he begins to pound on the outside of the garage entrance door. Wow, he finally realizes we aren't driving anymore.

"You're not coming in here, you betraying a—hole! Sleep outside!"

The pounding becomes a little stronger.

"I'm not letting you in, you f—ing a—hole! Go sleep with the little blonde. Jerk."

Now it gets fierce and I was even becoming a little scared. A little. I knew I had a man who would never be violent in any way, shape, or form to hurt me. But this doesn't sound good.

He breaks through the door.

Broke the door—a dead bolted door! Crazy.

So now it's the next day. I'm sure his head is pounding. He could hardly talk. And here I stand, waving a pair of scissors in his face, telling him how I am going to cut my wedding dress up into little pieces.

I tell him how I am going to destroy something that represents our bond, our beginning. I didn't think of the ring, the pictures, the marriage license. They all could have been equally useful in my coming metaphor, but I chose the dress to focus on. My beautiful, white, sequined, wedding dress. I wasn't sure why at the time.

Maybe I wanted to attack the dress because it represented *my* day. My day to be fabulously beautiful. The absolute center of everything. Someone making sure every hair was in place while someone else took pictures, while everyone around me became obsolete against my full white dress.

Here I was, receiving all the attention and focus I had been deprived of since my little sister was born. The day everyone surrounded the cute, new baby girl in her little bassinet and forgot about the scraggly little toddler looking only at knees. Maybe.

So here, on my wedding day, what seemed like a million years later, all eyes were fixed on me—and that dress.

I stood there with my scissors. *Oh, my Lord, does he even get it? Have you given me an ignorant man?*

He thinks I'm crazy. He thinks he didn't do anything to me. I explain to him what he did to me, and he doesn't believe that it was that big of a deal.

Sorry, sweetheart, but it was a huge deal. It wasn't your first and I learned later it certainly wasn't going to be your last.

THREE

~~~~~~~~~

I was an official mother. I had three children. I think motherhood becomes official after two. With one, you have yourself a little buddy, a partner, some little sweet thing to raise and hang out with you. Mothering comes in its purest sense when we become a referee, a judge, a jury, a cop, and whatever other description you may want to add. I could write pages filled with a mother's job description.

It's like a little world inside these four walls with the mommy being *everything* needed to run a world.

To run a world, you need population—at least two nations at odds with each other. Some world leaders are monitoring six or seven nations. God bless them.

And those jobs listed above are some of the worst jobs in the world. The judge, jury, referee. At least in my opinion. Having to monitor the arguing, whining, she did this, he did that, all in shrill voices that send a knife into your spine. And you have to participate, because they are always coming to *you* with one menial situation or another.

President, vice president, CIA, FBI, accountant, nutritionist, janitor, garbage collector. I could go on, but you get the idea. Well, all of us official mothers, of course, get the idea.

He, on the other hand, has no idea.

And I've established who *he* is, at least in my little world.

The father. The one who just goes to work in the morning, comes home to a meal and a little television, and plays with these little, clean, well-rested children, without a clue as to how they got that way.

And why is it they are so happy? Not fighting? Not screaming? They must hate me and somehow know I won't convince their father of any hell I went through to get us to five o'clock in the evening as he gazes into their sweet, lovely faces.

And I can't convince him. He hears my words, or at least nods his head once in a while. But he isn't going to believe me. That comes out later. The truth always comes out later. The words sneak into an argument. Words that imply my life is so easy. That *I* don't have to get up and go to work. This kills me. *That I don't have to go to work?*

I'm running a &*%#ing world here, you ignoramus!

Can't you see that I'm working hard to keep the peace between the nations? This is very stressful. Can you not see the worry that weighs on my heart as I work to keep out the terrorists, protecting the boundaries in which my little nations reside?

And what about the horror I deal with as I enter another part of our world, with toys strewn and clothes scattered, wiped out by some destructive hurricane that bears the name of one of our little children? And, baby, no Red Cross is coming to *my* rescue.

He sees the world as I, the president, stand and give my speech on the "state of our little world." But *he* has no idea of the work and stress, the heartache and torment that I go through when the cameras are not on, a.k.a when he's at work. It's a losing battle. One I choose not to fight any longer. He can believe his little tabloid lies about my easy, jobless life if he wants to. I know what I do, what I go through, and I don't need affirmation from anybody. Well, that line is untrue. Yeah, affirmation would be good. If I didn't need it, I wouldn't be so bitter.

FOUR

~~~~~~~~~~~~~

Years travel quickly. The nations mature, and as we train them to monitor themselves, a bit of freedom comes to motherhood. We come to a point where we can sleep in the morning knowing our children can feed themselves without pouring some poisonous liquid cleaner into their cereal bowl. Only a bit of freedom from monitoring the nations comes because there are occasional wars, and I don't believe these will ever end until I have an empty nest.

One particular night I felt I needed a night out of the house. The kids were wearing on my brain, I had written nothing for days, and, hey, the husband was going out without me, so why should I be stuck at home?

I called my beer-drinking-going-out girlfriend to see if she wanted to go out for a beer. I always called her when I wanted to go for a beer, 'cuz she likes to drink beer and if I call, chances are I have someone to go out and drink beer with.

She said, "Yeah, let's go out."

And I think, *I don't want to go sit in some bar and talk. I don't feel like talking.*

So I tell her, "I need to be entertained." Then I gave her three choices: comedy club, movie, or male dance show.

I really push the comedy club and movies. Here's why. I knew she wasn't going to drive across town to the comedy club. Besides, she really doesn't care for them, and she absolutely hates the movie theater. So by pushing these two, I don't look too desperate to see some bootie. It works, and we go to the guy show.

We're early; the place is practically empty. We slipped in, sat at the bar, and ordered our drinks. Her old dancer boyfriend walked up to us with a friend—another dancer guy. At first I didn't pay much attention. I wasn't really there to make new friends. Or talk to a guy.

The four of us began to chit-chat with each other about the show and whether the place would fill or not, small talk. The married thing didn't come up for a minute or two. While we chatted, this dancer guy looked directly at my hand and noticed I didn't wear a ring, so maybe he assumed for a moment I was available.

When my married status did come up, I may have surprised him, possibly disappointed him. Nonetheless, he and I kept talking as the two next to us caught up on old times. I think he may have spent those first minutes thinking he would take me to his passion palace.

That wasn't going to happen. I wasn't going anywhere with anyone. I walked into this place a fully married mommy, and I intended to leave that way.

Except for one problem.

This guy was *dang* good.

FIVE

~~~~~~~~~~

I can't believe I lost my cigarette lighter again. I haven't even gone anywhere, although I am in my car. It's my nice little office. Soft leather seats I can position just so until I find the highest level of comfort. A CD player so I can play all my songs that take me to places only I know about and can find.

And I can smoke in here.

Where is that lighter? There are lots of little places for it to fall into. I have a very messy office.

Once, I studied personalities for an obsessive three days of my life. I read that to identify someone of my personality, look for a messy car. That's what I got out of three days. But it was very freeing. It was a great aha! moment in my life. I no longer fight it. I no longer stress when I clean my car thoroughly only to find it messy again in two days.

It's just me. A messy car is just a strangely marked piece of my very complicated make-up.

I call these complications trade-offs. They are spectacular personality things that must go together, the bad held hand-in-hand with its opposite, positive counterpart. For example, if the ability to express myself were in direct relation to having a messy car and the messy car were a manifestation of my self-expression, to fight the less desirable would also be fighting the desirable. If I fought my messy car, I may fight my ability to express myself.

Fighting or hating myself because of undesirable qualities causes frustration, disturbance, and may even result in possibly losing the desirable, which, for me, would not be an option.

The most amazing part of this is, when you embrace the undesirable in your self, your life, and you begin to express the desirable quality, your undesirable partner to this quality begins to fade. And in opposition to this, it's as if the less you express the desirable, the more the undesirable is magnified.

I've always said that I believe the pleasure I can experience in life is in direct relation to the amount of pain I have experienced. Pretend life is a water pitcher. A water pitcher can only be filled up to the proportion in which it can be emptied. My pleasure can be filled only to the depth that my pain has caused its emptiness.

We all need to see who we are. Really see. The good and the bad, and even that the bad leads to the good, if you try to understand it that way.

When we try to suppress who we are, especially the bad stuff that we don't want anyone to know about, we also inhibit the very opposite positive qualities we posses.

This is what I did in my marriage. I put away all the bad stuff I didn't want anyone to know about. And, in the process, I could not experience the very opposite of that pain, the pleasure. I held back my ability to share the truth about my pain, and thus never confronting it, never doing anything about it, I never found a way to open my doors to pleasure. I suppressed how absolutely unhappy I was and thus stifled feeling any real happiness anywhere in my life for a very, very long time.

The water pitcher was empty (the pain), but I didn't confront the empty water pitcher (the pain). I ignored it. I smiled to let everyone believe it was full (the pleasure). I even deceived myself into believing it was full (the pleasure). Had I been honest with myself, and allowed myself to confront all of the bad stuff (the pain), I would then have been free to deal with the pain and do something about it. But I didn't.

I always put on such a good front. Anyone who knew us throughout the years would be surprised my husband and I had not even kissed in years.

Years.

Only when I became truthful with myself and the idea of writing about a decade of marriage, as I sat down to really vent my true unhappiness and confront my empty water pitcher, only then did I discover my desperate need to allow joy to enter my soul.

SIX

~~~~~~~~~~~~~~~~~

I was hit. Unexpectedly. This night out. This dancer guy's words. For some reason they reached into a place within me no one has gone before—at least not in a long, long time. And he knew it. He saw it in my eyes. It kept him here, to see what was going to happen next.

This dancer guy just split up from a seven-year relationship and with that I find myself pretty lucky. I have this rebounding, hot, fantasy dancer guy all to myself for one fantasy night out. He's whispering sweet things in my ear, rubbing my back.

He was good. Funny, I didn't know I wanted to be touched by someone, until he touched me, and I didn't know I wanted a strange man in my space, until he was close to me.

At the time I thought I was having an uneventful conversation with another person. I had no idea what was taking place under the surface, deep within me.

Fantasy dancer guy asked if we could have an affair, and I laughed. I would not even think of doing such a thing. I'd blown off other offers throughout my decade of marriage. It just wasn't something I was into. I didn't ever look at other men to entertain thoughts of fooling around with them. I didn't come to this place to find a man to fool around with. Coming to this dance club was about spending time with the girls and seeing a show. I was very committed to my married mommy status, no matter how crazy it drove me sometimes. But this was super flattering, even from a male dancer slut who probably proposed such a thing to as many women as I could imagine. Regardless, I let myself be flattered.

Actually, I really didn't think he was a slut. He seemed to have had some very long, very committed relationships.

But even if he were, what makes him different from the jerk who flies around the world screwing different girls in every city he visits on his business trips?

Ah, yeah. There's where society can't judge. I could have some suited up business guy, head of a corporation or something, professional, and hitting on me, and I could have no idea he screws everyone he meets. This way, because there won't be an affair anyway, it doesn't matter to me if this fantasy dancer guy has many affairs or sleeps around or not.

I've got some beautiful babe of a fantasy standing next to me, gorgeous thick black hair with soft eyes and amazing lips. Blue jeans shaped perfectly around his tight waist and sweet butt, hiding not much of his bulging, hard thighs, and resting ever so lightly at his ankles. His tight red shirt clinging desperately to his very fine cut upper body and arms with hard-core fantasy guy tattoos that drew my eyes to meet the most amazing sculpted piece of flesh this little suburbia momma had seen in a long time.

This man was a molded piece of work for the eyes to behold—a heavenly creation who made me smile. Way better than a stuffy old suit. I wouldn't want to imagine what the suit could be hiding.

With him, this fantasy dancer guy, I didn't have to guess on anything. Well, almost anything. And if I'm going to have a fantasy guy, which I didn't know I was until the next day, then *he* was absolutely perfect.

SEVEN

~~~~~~~~

I'm in my car, my little office-in-the-garage, my place to write and smoke, and I just had dinner delivered by my husband, delivered with a scowl and a slam of the door. He hates that I write. I'm not cooking dinner, the house isn't clean, everyone's laundry gets put off in the name of creative inspiration.

I became a kind of wife he wasn't accustomed to when I started pursuing passions in my life. My husband hates my passions—they didn't make money, pay the bills, and they consumed my time. Hmmm, neither did his passions.

He hates that I write, but I feel like it's me he hates. I do sometimes think I may be turning into a terrible wife and mother, more like the one I was raised by, more concern for herself than her home and children. I've worked my butt off, though, for ten years doing this job. Can I never tire of it? Does that make me a terrible wife and mother if I tire of these repeated duties?

I don't mind the duties terribly. I just need a small distraction—a bit of excitement—something to remind me that I am living a real life here, one of value.

I feel I'm suddenly coming to life, coming to terms with whom I want to be and what I want to do. And sometimes people don't like it when you step outside of the box—outside of your box, the one *they* have designed for you, the one they are used to seeing you in, the one they expect to keep you in.

It is hard to be brave enough to say, "No, I will not conform to whom you think I should be. I'm going to be true to myself, and if you don't like the real me, for me, then it's your problem, not mine."

It seems it makes no difference to my husband I have put an incredibly dedicated ten years of my life into keeping these small people alive and well, and this one big one clothed and fed.

Now, I am moving into a new place and it is very uncomfortable to him. And, of course, he would hate me. This is not the kind of wife and mother he has seen before. His model was of a quite wonderful mother—one I tried to keep up with, but couldn't.

It took me ten years to realize my house doesn't need to be spotless; flowers don't need to be planted everywhere, every spring; to realize walls don't need to be painted quarterly, and windows washed bimonthly. Ten years it took me to wake up and say, "Screw this, I'm going to do something more, something of meaning, and something of value."

My next ten years are going to kick butt. I'm going to do those things that, when remembered, are going to excite me all over again. As I lie upon my deathbed and ponder the days I have lived, what I have done, I guarantee I won't give a single thought to my smudged walls and smeared windows.

This excites me. It's like I can find freedom on the horizon. Something absolutely magnificent to chase after. I see it out there. Now I'm running.

Now I'm kickin' butt.

EIGHT

I think glue, married people hanging out with married people, is good for a marriage. I married into a large group of my husband's friends who were married and marrying. They're a group that contains characters and characteristics of all sorts.

We have the sexy jock type and his cute blonde cheerleader wife, just like I always would have imagined Barbie and Ken in real life. You gotta love them; they are beautiful people.

We have the poor ones who can't stop complaining about being poor, and we have the rich ones, with the big house and the perfect little Christmas pictures with the little girls in velvet dresses and ruffles, their Christmas notes always arriving on time, I might add. Mine are always late, and that's if I even send them.

We have the naked friends. The ones you imagine retiring on a nude beach somewhere—the sex fiends, naked and having sex all of the time. A lot of us should be jealous. We talk, and a lot of us aren't having sex like that. We really like our naked friends because we all know we *should* be having sex like that.

We have the childless friends. They're the ones who really can suck sometimes—always going out to do the fun things, like vacations and dinners out, we parent couples can't do without it costing a fortune for a babysitter and using up the money we really need for lunch tickets.

And the list goes on.

All are very amazing people, all in their own ways. There has been very little divorce in our group of friends. We have a central group of about fifteen couples that can expand on occasion to about twenty-five. Out of the fifteen, I'd say there has been one divorce, and out of the twenty-five, there are only two that I know of.

I have always found that level of commitment to be completely amazing, and it has caused me to believe that when you have incredible couple support amongst friends, it helps you to enjoy your marriage better. It gives you good examples of families who are able to pull through the hard times and find the good. It has possibly helped me get through ten years of marriage. There are some in the group I love, whom I would hate to be separated from.

I have to laugh, though, because I have no idea if all of these people really want to be married, let alone married to each other. I don't know what happens behind closed doors. I sometimes wonder, will the statistics sneak into this group someday? And then I wonder, which couple would be first? I always thought it might be my husband and me. I'm not quite sure why, when we seemed to appear one of the happiest. Maybe I knew something no one else did.

We have many amusing little jokes in our little group of friendships—great times of great joy in our young lives and marriages.

We had the surprise birthday at the naked people's house when, surprise, surprise, the birthday boy unwrapped a strip dart game that we all played after we were thoroughly hammered. Most of us weren't prepared for this. One was.

She had on a gold metallic bra and matching gold undies. Amazing, she looked great taking her clothes off. Of course, she was the one who bought the gift and was ready to strip. She could have called and given the rest of us a clue.

I vowed to never wear boring white cotton underwear from that day forward. But I do anyway.

It was very difficult to be liked within this close-knit group of my husband's friends. They didn't take well to "new blood." Slowly I made my way. They fell sort of in between the family/friend thing. Your family members are people you *have* to be around. You don't choose them. They were forced into your life by means other than selection. And most of them would have never been selected, had you even been given the choice. Sometimes our families are made up of people who are critical and negative; sometimes being around them is torture—even moments around them drag you down.

Then you have "your chosen."

These are people you cherish being with, every word and every moment. There is somehow never enough time in your life to be with these people. Even a lot of time is not always enough time. It's very tragic to have time stripped from you because it's spent with those you would not even choose to be with. Tragic to use up time better spent elsewhere, like time with "your chosen."

My husband's friends fell somewhere in between my forced and chosen. Most I enjoyed spending time with, but, along the lines of the forced, as with family, some of these friends had the ability to subject me to torture.

An example was an occasion to make money for an upcoming event—in a bar, a beer bust thing. And my husband and his friends were all getting extremely intoxicated. My husband of a short year was working closely with one of his big boobed female friends.

This, the first time I was his pregnant, fat, extremely self conscious sober cabbie, taking his drunken butt home.

I put him to bed like a loving, understanding wife would. I climbed in next to him and cuddled close. He must have appreciated it because he rolled his head back and said, "I love you," and, as his head moved back to the pillow, he said the big boobed girl's name.

He used her name! I love you, *her name?*

I wanted to kick his stupid drunk a—. He doesn't even know who he's in bed with? His $%^#ing wife? Carrying his first child?

I didn't kick his butt. I just rolled over.

It came out at our next gathering. I think I might have brought this on myself, made a comment like, the butthead didn't even buy me roses the next day, and with that, it became a familiar little joke in our little crowd of friends. Over time, I had gotten very sick of the little "I love you" joke, especially when *she* had to tell it.

That night I was mad about his "I love you, her name." Only that night, because, in spite of how humiliating it felt, I chose to be strong. And I would save pieces of myself, and hide them— from him, from me, from everyone around us.

NINE

~~~~~~~~~~

I blew off these many little betrayals, as I saw them. For the most part, I just lived with them, tucked them deep, and moved on. I thought.

I guess I needed to adjust to living with a man who wasn't just focused on me, his wife. I wasn't sure if there was any man out there just focused on his wife. I convinced myself these little betrayals were normal—normal marriage stuff. But why then did these things hurt so bad? Was I somehow setting myself up for disappointment thinking my man should be fully and solely focused on just me?

Now I understand it this way. The credit goes to my neighbor. This is her explanation, whether she made it up or read it, I'm not sure, but it makes complete sense and helps me to understand a lot of years of bitterness in a decade of marriage.

We all have emotional bank accounts, with our boyfriends, our spouses, friends, maybe even kids. I'm going to focus on the spouse thing.

Anyway, we have an emotional bank account. We get deposits and we get withdrawals. She explains it this way. When someone puts a lot of dimes and quarters into your emotional bank account over time, you don't feel it when they make a ten-dollar withdrawal.

It works like this. He brings home flowers—a dime. He runs a bubble bath—a nickel. Tells you how beautiful you are—a quarter. A brush of his hand to your face with a deep longing drink from your eyes—another quarter. On and on the deposits come until you're rattling around with change piled to your neck. Then, unexpectedly, he gets wasted and forgets you exist for a moment, grabs some girl's boob, and cha-ching, a twenty-dollar withdrawal is made. But wait a minute. If this guy has hundreds of dollars worth of dimes and quarters invested into his woman's bank account, what's twenty bucks?

This, I believe, is the key, the answer as to why we stay in a relationship or not. What does the account really look like? We all know women who stay with men and we know some of the crap the men are doing to their women. Why does she stay? She stays for the dimes and quarters, of course. She becomes addicted to the deposits and doesn't feel the withdrawals.

I maybe got two quarters and a few dimes deposited into my emotional bank account in ten years. And there *were* huge withdrawals, one after the other. My bank account was severely overdrawn.

I did my thing being mother and wife, and did a damn good job of it considering how hard of a job it really is. I always tried to be good to this man I was married to. I took good care of his house and his children, and took a heck of a ride in my own life while I was doing it.

I was changing. Discovering. I wanted my life to be better than it was. I was tired of hurting. This man, my husband, was livid with my affairs, my church affairs. He hated when

I left to go to church. He hated when I came home from church happy.

And all this anger toward me, when he was the one who always took off on hunting trips, fishing trips, the bars. He was leaving me with the babies weekend after weekend, his single friends chiding in his ears about how a woman shouldn't *control* what he did. He listened to them, left with them, all of the time, without looking back.

Staying home with your family shouldn't have been about control. It should have been about love and devotion to the one you married. Had he looked back, he would have seen the tears, tears that had names. Worthlessness. Uselessness. Rejection. Betrayal. Abandonment.

I constantly stood there in my home, feeling deserted and forsaken. Now it was my turn and he was so angry, feeling deserted and forsaken.

Still I went. If there was a service, I was going to it. At least when I was in church, I didn't hate my life. It gave me hope.

He hated it, hated I was living differently. He stuck around, but tormented me.

He stuck around, kept up the happy marriage facade with me.

I was in church, reading the Bible, praising the Lord. I was happy for once, and there were worse things I could have been doing. It was good for me.

He didn't care. It wasn't good for him. He yelled at me. Made fun of me. Gave me dirty looks. Hated me.

I was strong. I was happy. But every day I cried for him, for my marriage.

TEN

~~~~~~~~~~~~~~~

Colored lights flew across the stage while the silver glitter disco ball cast little white dots over all the faces. The loud music filled the club. An emcee announced the next dancer's appearance on stage. Women screamed on cue. I had a few drinks, which were plenty for a light weight like me. I didn't drink much, so even a little bit of alcohol brought me to a state I wasn't used to. I didn't pay much attention to the show, or I just don't remember—an alcohol inflicted slip of memory.

I do know this dancer guy spent most of the show hanging around me, talking, trying to push the affair proposal. *Funny thing is,* I thought, *if I was going to have an affair, which I wasn't, I sure wouldn't pick it with some guy that knows his stuff like this.*

I'm thinking, *can you imagine the girls this guy has taken his clothes off for and how many chicks he's put his you-know-what into?* I had really convinced myself this guy had male dancer slut written all over him.

When I can't control a judging thought like that, I sit on it. Who am I to say what he does or has done? I am an empathy person. I want your story first. I'm not a critical, it's either black or white, type person. I believe in gray. I'm just waiting to give you grace and mercy for what you do or have done. After all,

I am no innocent bystander here. I had my days. I understand stupid crap. If everyone would think about it, they'd realize they understand stupid crap, too. The only reason they judge it, and point at it, is they don't want anyone to see their own stupid crap.

They think, *if I say that person is doing something wrong, then the people around me will think that I've never done anything wrong like that.* This is called stupid crap denial and is judgment in its strongest form. Or, they think, *if I call this person an idiot, then everyone will think I'm somehow above doing that and thus, I am no idiot.* When in fact, you *are* exactly what you name and judge someone else for. You fear in yourself what you are judging in others and denying in your own life. Oh, how this lesson has come to me the hard way, but what an incredible, freeing lesson it is.

Think about that the next time you judge. Your every judgment on someone else is a characteristic inside of you. Your judgment is about something you are hiding, from yourself and from the world, something far larger than what you find appalling in the person you are judging.

If someone judges, it is *their* issue. If you judge, it is *your* issue. No ifs, ands, or buts, it is about you.

If something bothers you about someone, ask yourself why you are so bothered, ask yourself why it is your business to monitor someone else's life, especially if that person's life does not directly affect your own. You will be miserable for as long as you are pointing at someone else's life and refusing to look at your own.

Our life is about ourselves, about bringing ourselves to the highest level of understanding, acceptance, and love of others.

This message of what's my business and what's not became loud and clear as I progressed through my relationship with this fantasy dancer guy. My judgments confront me. My hate confronts me. My pointing finger turns to myself.

My biggest lesson happened with my mother. And, in a month's time, I learned, I wasn't so mad at her for what she was doing in her marriages. I held despair in myself, because I shouldn't do in my life what she had done in hers.

On the surface I hated that my mother left marriages she was unhappy in, because deep down I knew I wanted to leave mine, but I couldn't.

ELEVEN

～～～～～～

There was a point in our wedded bliss, this being about the eighth year, my husband and I were getting along great. It was the height and the depth of our marriage. And it lasted almost a week.

One week.

Every day for a week we were doing what maybe you would think only hot passionate lovers do. All barriers were down, and we just couldn't get enough of each other.

I was famous for my emotional walls. Pain caused me to put them up, and I was very careful about whom I allowed beyond those walls.

Our passionate lover's episode was a week of heaven on earth. This was what marriage is supposed to be like. Sharing your bed with someone you really actually *want* to be there, happy to jump in and rip your clothes off. Leave the lights on. Explore hidden places. Sleep in the wet spot. All while loving each other in the permissive bond of marriage. It doesn't get much better.

This started on Sunday. All day Sunday, twice on Monday, once on Tuesday, some more on Wednesday, an hour's worth on Thursday, again Friday morning, and then I had an appointment.

The yearly visit to the gynecologist's office is what I had scheduled for this particular morning. This routine visit doesn't bother me much. I adore my doctor. He makes the exam pain-less and there's not much embarrassment since we've been together, doctor and patient, for ten years and two babies.

I was waiting in his office, sitting there naked under a paper sheet for over an hour. And I wasn't mad. I understood because my doctor was delivering a baby. I opted to wait so I could get this thing over with.

By the time I was done, it was lunch time. I thought, *I'll deliver my wonderful spouse a nice meal at his jobsite.*

He squirmed in the car. He was uncomfortable. He had told himself earlier there was no way I would be in the area for lunch, considering my morning appointment. But if I was, he would confess to me the guilt he's carried with his miser-able, rotten, haunting memory of sex and betrayal. And his alibi would be there with him—a night of drunkenness, a party, and @#$%ed-up pornographic sex at our naked friends' house.

And where was I when this happened? I had taken the kids on a nice little family trip to *his* mother's house in Florida. The height and the breadth of our marriage was over. Lasting just short of a week—one week in ten years.

The construction started again and another wall went up.

And I wouldn't kiss him after his day of confession, not ever again.

TWELVE

~~~~~~~~~~~~

Daily life was always challenging, but it became a real struggle from his confession day on. I was dedicated to the vow I made so many years before, and I stayed with the father of my children. But, secretly, I hated him. I didn't let it show too much. I just went about my married mommy life.

I cleaned the house. I did the laundry. I washed windows, mowed the grass, and painted walls. I did everything I could think of, doing things to pass my days and not allow me to feel. Waiting for the day...

Hmmm, actually, I don't know what I was waiting for. I look at it now, and I see it as if I were waiting out a prison term. Day after day, duties—lifeless, feeling-less duties. Wake up. Do the married mommy thing. And go to sleep. All the while waiting for the day when one of us would disappear. *'Til death do us part.* I was waiting for the day I would be set free. And with dedication to my vows and determination in commitment, death was my only way out.

Sometimes we have no idea what we are missing if we haven't experienced "the thing." We can hear about a thing and have an idea of it, maybe even quite an appealing idea, of what something may be like. But, until we experience it, fully experience it, life can pass us by without us even knowing it exists.

Sometimes it can be safer this way. I spent ten years, since my husband threatened me during our wedding dance, not allowing myself to feel (as far as a relationship) anything with a man. I watched movies with a wall up. I listened to music with a wall up. I looked at pictures with a wall. I read with a wall. I wrote with a wall.

It was safe this way, so I, in the very depths of myself, would protect myself from what my life was, (full of pain) and what I wouldn't let myself believe was available to me (freedom from the pain). The freedom was unavailable because I made a vow, a vow to myself, to my husband, and before God. 'Til death do us part.

And because of this vow, and the pain that came with this vow, I retreated and would not allow myself to feel. I went to sleep, but it was not an apple from a witch that put me in my coma. It was a wall. My wall. The wall my husband forced me to construct to protect myself. And I fell very soundly asleep behind it.

Until someone woke me up.

An amazing someone.

THIRTEEN

~~~~~~~~~~

I woke up in the morning after the night out at the guy show and went about my day. But the tasks didn't catch my attention. I was stirring, so I figured I would get out of the house. I tried a couple of errands, and then decided to just go park my car. I chose a spot in a lot far from any other cars or any people who would witness my strangeness. I put my hand on the seat controls and adjusted myself to the perfect position of extreme comfort. I cranked the tunes, lay back, and let the images of fantasy dancer guy roll around inside of me.

I thought about fantasy dancer guy's words. His voice ran through my veins into the very depths of my soul. His hands remained ghostly upon my shoulders; his breath lingered in my ear. I could somehow smell him around me as if I had carried his presence with me from the night before. I didn't know this man before yesterday, yet I somehow felt as if I had known him forever. Who was he, and how did he get through my wall?

Now, I'm thinking, I'm not completely stupid. I have spent years getting my head on straight, being a very balanced and logical person. I ran a little world here, remember, and did a pretty darn good job at it. My world looked good to everyone around me. I had a long lasting marriage, and well-behaved children with good grades, and offered respectful empathy toward the elders and friends. I had a business I was doing well with.

I wasn't quite sure what was going on inside me. Why was I being touched by a guy like this? But I wasn't going to give it too much thought, and I sure wasn't going to talk to anyone about it. I would remain within the fantasy in my head and keep it to myself as I savored every moment of what I was experiencing.

I let fantasy dancer guy's presence do what I needed it to do. I went home and completed a screenplay I was writing. With that done, I still had all this stuff inside of me, words, thoughts, passion, and pain, coming up out of me, crying to be released, so I did what any aspiring writer would do when something is very intensely touching the deep places within themselves. I wrote. And I was very impressed with what was coming out, so I kept this stirring fantasy going until I couldn't go anymore.

A whole month went by; I finished a screenplay, wrote one book, and started a second. My husband just left for another guy's weekend when I was cleaning out my purse and came across a piece of paper. I unfolded it. I pondered how this little slip of paper got into my purse as read his name, the number, and the little message written on it. I start thinking of him again, my fantasy dancer guy, what he did to me, how he made me feel.

FOURTEEN

~~~~~~~~~

I know he told me to call him if I wanted to have an affair. I didn't call for that reason, or at least I didn't *think* that was why I called. I asked him if I could call for a non-affair. He said, "Yeah." I'm sure he was trying to figure out how to take the "non" out of it.

I met him that same night. I took a friend, my neighbor, someone I thought I could trust to help me through seeing him again, help me to understand. This friend is quite beyond the picture you may be drawing. She's a military, suburbia, married mommy who has been through stuff. She's well read in the self help area and that was enough for me to qualify her as my official on-call, neighbor-therapist. She knew stuff I didn't know, learned stuff I had yet to encounter.

I met her when my husband and I picked out land to build our house on. We bought a half acre extension from their lot. The price was right and our kids were all the same ages. It seemed perfect.

From the beginning, we had conversations beyond the normal surface ones, and these conversations grew as years passed. It didn't bother us we had very different religious beliefs; there were so many other subjects we could explore and share. I guess I should say it bothered her less.

We laugh about the time she and I were talking shortly after my husband and I purchased the land. I was out walking it, taking in the hill, chatting about how the house will be placed. She made a comment she believed we knew each other in a past life. Past life? What?

She laughs hysterically when she pictures the strict Christian reaction on my face. I laugh hysterically when I remember how horrified I was that this was my new neighbor. Nonetheless, we have been able to carry on a friendship—a needed friendship, for this time, which would help me to immensely understand some key points in my search for meaning through my uncontrollable, intense interest in fantasy dancer guy.

FIFTEEN

~~~~~~~~~

My therapist-neighbor-friend and I had a nice drive as we sneaked out to a little out-of-town bar so I could once again get my high from fantasy dancer guy. She and I would talk about anything and everything. I can't remember exactly what the conversation was on this particular drive. I was pretty anxious to get my fix.

And my fix I got. The dancer guys were just finishing up the show. I didn't pay too much attention. This trip had not much to do with seeing the guy in his underwear, although he did look so, so fine.

He really got to me with his clothes on.

Tonight he looked like something out of the recesses of my wildest, deepest, darkest most hidden imaginations of a fantasy guy. How could a living human being look like this? And do what he did to me?

My mind continued to go completely wild.

Uncontrollable passionate longing rose in certain parts of me, not necessarily the parts you may be thinking of. I think this was much deeper than that, deeper than just lust. Maybe, I just can't define what I felt.

I kept reminding myself of my suburbia married momma condition and that is who I needed to remain. But this wasn't about sex. I did know that. This wasn't about running off with fantasy dancer guy. It was something else—something I hadn't identified yet—so I let myself stay in my mind. I was having the time of my life there. This just didn't feel like what I thought lust felt like—unless I have never really lusted before. I thought I had, but I guess I can't really say. If I hadn't lusted before, I wouldn't be able to identify it, would I? But wouldn't lust point to sex? And I didn't want to have sex with him.

I did think about running off with him. Of course I played out that fantasy in my mind. *Three and a half weeks*, I thought, *lying in the sand somewhere, with the hot sun beating upon our flesh. That's all I want, three and a half weeks to run off to some remote sandy beach somewhere with the mass of ocean surrounding us...*

Or just me. Me with my laptop.

That's where the revelation came in. I was talking about it with my therapist-neighbor-friend. I asked her, "*Did I say me?*"

Could it be possible I could run away to the beach just as passionately without the man, with just my laptop?

That is what I said.

I would hang out on the beach with my computer, get away from it all, and be with myself, and my passion.

So if I could run away with my passion to write, maybe all this stirring that fantasy dancer was causing in me wasn't about my intense attraction to fantasy dancer guy.

I ask, "Why then? Why does it seem on the outside that my interest is in him?"

She looked at me and stated simply that it was about what the guy represented that I wanted for my life.

What?

I'm thinking this is incredible insight. What she said made sense. I was at a time in my life when I was trying to figure it all out, trying to break free from the mundane life I had created for myself. I had been trying to write for years, never coming up with anything that really worked, that felt right. I knew what I wanted to do, but it was buried far too deep beneath my suburbia married mommy exterior.

I was stuck in a house taking care of kids. He was working in an exciting atmosphere, the lights, the music, the laughter. I was looking at the same faces, talking to the same people day after day, for years. Every night for him was a new crowd, changed faces, new possibilities. My day went predictably, as I performed my duties. The most action packed thing in my day was a kid wiped out on the bike or something.

Day after day the same in my life.

And that is why I allowed myself to be drawn to him.

He had what I did not have. He had freedom. And if I could keep my head together on this thing, for I already had a man in my bed, I had that part, this wasn't about sleeping with him, but as long as I could keep it together, I could use this to understand what it is I need to seek out in myself and how to get what I need, without tearing my family apart.

I knew deep down inside that this guy was a key. I just needed to find out exactly what door that key was going to unlock. Did I *need* to run away to get what I so longed for? What if I couldn't get what I needed *without* running away?

Discovering the first answer was the easy part thanks to my therapist-neighbor-friend. The next part was going to be the real challenge—a challenge because now I know why I am attracted to him, I just have to figure out what I'm going to do with the attraction.

SIXTEEN

~~~~~~~~~~

Fantasy dancer guy has really experienced quite a wild life. Try to imagine the clubs and the shows, all-night parties, road trips, drugs, sex, and all of the above as much as you want, or don't want, right at the fingertips. He has pretty full access to amazing girls who work hard to keep themselves beautiful and in form. This is a different world these people are living in. Seductive. Sexy. Free. Far from the suburbia life I was living in.

My world consisted of mini van driving McDonald's moms and their crying, screaming kids in booster chairs shoving French fries into their snot-filled faces, and moms and dads at soccer games arguing about which kid should be playing and which kid should be sitting, solving the world's greatest problems.

My life, I am sick of it. Not that I want to leave it forever or anything like that. I adore being a wife and mother. For the most part, I get great joy out of this aspect of my life, and I wouldn't change it for anything. My beautiful family is a huge part of my beautiful life.

I am just so sick of such trivial daily chores being all there is in my life. I want more and I want out. Somehow, some way, I want there to be more meaning and deeper purpose. I'm just not happy with every day being about kids, cleaning, cooking, and going to bed, with the only thing to look forward to is yet another day all about the same.

My trivial life, absent of meaning and purpose, was paralyzing me. It sometimes caused me to fantasize about the oak tree in the back yard, a rope, and my death.

I need to get away. I need to go somewhere very far away from this life, this trivial, meaningless, boring, mundane life.

But I knew it wasn't another man's bed I needed to go to. As appealing as the thought was, it would be momentary, fleeting, and it wasn't going to fulfill whatever it was I needed for the long term, for a real change.

My wake-up call was not about needing him, fantasy dancer guy, to whisk me off, out of my dull, boring suburbia life. It was really about what fantasy dancer guy could bring *into* my life. I desperately needed *something* from this man. I just wasn't exactly sure what it was.

I only knew the part it wasn't.

I needed to hang out with this guy. I needed answers. This was beyond what I could control and it wasn't about hurting anyone.

I went to another one of fantasy dancer guy's shows. I went alone so I could just sit and observe for a while. And I could observe, and did observe, as much as I could while some lesbian, or whatever she was, was working to pick me up. I don't think she came for the guys. I think she came for the bar full of women.

Anyway, I watched all of the women, yelling, screaming, cheering for these guys, all of these fantasy dancer guys. I don't think one woman did not have a smile on her face.

I thought, *where do they come from? What brings them here?* Were they too coming from boring humdrum lives to experience moments of freedom, excitement, and fantasy?

They come. They laugh. They enjoy. Then the show ends. And they go home. Did they leave the fantasy behind to return to their boring, humdrum lives?

Maybe not. Maybe they take a piece home with them, and bring a little excitement, freedom, and fantasy into their own lives. Maybe this would be my own destiny with fantasy dancer guy. Maybe this show would also end. And if it were to ever end, which I really didn't want the show to ever end, but if it were to end, could I take some of what he has given to me and incorporate it into my own life?

SEVENTEEN

~~~~~~~~~~

I woke one morning without any thought to the marriage bed I was sleeping in and my husband of ten years occupying the other half. I lay there next to my husband with secret thoughts of my fantasy dancer guy.

It seemed I could sense things about fantasy dancer guy. I spent some time talking with him and really did believe that he was a very thoughtful, caring, loving, faithful person caught up in a world he could not control. Only he could verify that, but he had given me nothing to believe he wasn't the loyal, sweet person he appeared to be.

And if he isn't, and wasn't, it does not matter to me. I need to get what I need. What am *I* doing? Maybe there are things *I'm* not telling him.

He tells me he doesn't want to get caught up with me. He's afraid to get wrapped up in this thing; I say my marriage is happy. He tells me it would be a different story if I wasn't happy. "But," he asks, "if you are so happy, what are you calling me for?" This is a good question. Why would I claim to be happy in my marriage, yet allow myself to be attracted to someone else? This, I had yet to discover.

Back to that morning. The morning I woke up thinking about him. I felt my heart turn. At that point, I didn't care who he was. He was on my A list. And nothing he could do or say could shock me. I didn't care. I saw him differently.

That morning, fantasy dancer guy took a piece of my heart, and I literally felt it. I know exactly where and when it happened. Don't get this wrong, I have female friends who have a piece of my heart, as do my kids, my mother, my sister.

This heart thing wasn't about sex. We can't make everything about sex. As a matter of a fact, it felt so much deeper than sex.

It was more like this man was pointing at my water pitcher, my empty water pitcher, the pitcher I pretended was full, told everyone was full. Remember, I told him my marriage was happy. But somehow, I couldn't pretend with him. He pointed to the empty pitcher, the pain I held, and I couldn't ignore it. I couldn't deceive myself any longer, nor deny the pain my marriage brought to me.

Sometimes we hide from ourselves, afraid of what we will find, terrified at what road we are on, horrified to find ourselves in a state of being which is far from where we ever wanted to be. And we remain in denial, and ignore our lost dreams and hopes. Sometimes we settle for less than our childhood dreams. The majority of us never become who our deep inner spirit wants us to become. Some of us become someone we never wanted to become. No one decides one day, I want to have a drug addiction, or I want to abuse my child, or I want to have a dead marriage. They are horrors that slip into our lives slowly, drip by drip, week by week.

Then one day we wake up and see our true state. We are given an opportunity to seize this realization and do something about it, to confront we are not the person we were to become, or we became quite opposite of who we thought we should be.

This realization is an opportunity presented to you to begin your self-relationship, self-acceptance, self-love process. You begin first by being attracted to yourself, and then actually become very excited about being with yourself. You start having conversations and meetings with yourself. You enjoy and look forward to the possibilities and the potential for yourself.

You gain confidence in your ability to learn, change, grow and release who you are not and become who you truly want to be.

This meeting and these feelings were about myself, about deciding it was time to stop denying the pain and ignoring the empty water pitcher. Finally it was time for *my* dance with my life, my dance with my destiny.

These days became the days I analyzed who I really am, who I have become, who I will be. Meeting fantasy dancer guy revealed the truth beneath every facade I placed in my life. These days became the days I, for once, found myself embracing everything, my faults, my shortcomings. During this time I uncovered my psuedo life and found true freedom.

I want the dance. I need the dance. Please don't tear me from *this* dance.

EIGHTEEN

~~~~~~~~~~~

I had another therapy session. The self help lessons came pouring in and great psychological revelations were opening my universe. My therapist-neighbor-friend, once again, went over what this guy stood for in my life, and, as we hashed it out, our conversation revealed more to me.

He, fantasy dancer guy, was sexy, free, spontaneous, adventurous, and brave. He had to be, doing what he was doing. "And here he is," she said, "taking it all off, exposing himself for hundreds of people."

She looked at me.

"That takes courage," she went on, "to be able to bear yourself like that in front of so many people."

Her brows rise when she stated simply and matter-of-factly, "And what is it you want to do with your life?"

I was speechless. There it was. I mean I didn't want to take my clothes off in front of anybody, but bear my self, yes, in a way. My soul, maybe. I wanted to talk about things no one else wanted to talk about. Go places no one else wanted to go. My writing flowed best when I talked about myself, my life. But I didn't think I would really ever be brave enough to put all this stuff out there.

It's one thing to write about some false fiction thing and have people hate it, but it is far different to write about your most intimate depths and put it out there to be scrutinized and criticized.

In a way, this is what fantasy dancer guy did every time he worked throughout his thirteen-year career. He took his clothes off and bore some of his most intimate details. And, depending on the crowd, he put himself out there to be scrutinized, criticized.

Of course, we are always our biggest critic, our biggest scrutinizer. And he was pretty safe. Ninety-nine percent of these people, 99 percent of the time wanted to be there. They wanted to see him, wanted him to take his clothes off, and they are welcoming and open.

I have spent my life walking in fear of that 1 percent.

I know most of us fear that 1 percent.

That 1 percent who will tell us we are not good enough, that we are wrong.

That 1 percent was holding me back from my dreams and aspirations.

I need to take unspoken advice from my fantasy dancer guy and say, "Screw the 1 percent. I'm dancing for my ninety-nine."

Oh my God, help me. I swear, I have fallen in love with him and this is an incredible thing for me, because we know I possibly couldn't have fallen in love with fantasy dancer guy in such a short time. I haven't. More accurately, I have fallen in love with the idea of fantasy dancer guy *within me*. I have fallen in love with the *possibility* of fantasy dancer guy within me, with the idea and the possibility of chasing after my dreams and goals, forging ahead without fear, and going after that which I can. Dancing. For my ninety-nine.

NINETEEN

~~~~~~~~~

So is it possible? Is this idea of my fantasy dancer guy attraction solely about my desires for my life outside of the man? And if it is, could it work for others, too? Could the separated lady that moved in down the street have avoided leaving her husband if she had a fantasy dancer guy and a great-neighbor-friend-therapist?

A bunch of us sat out at a neighborhood bon fire. Our new neighbor was rattling on about the man who now occupied her couch. She called him antisocial and lazy, or something like that. I don't usually recall someone's exact words, just pictures or paraphrases. Antisocial and lazy, is what I recall. And this was the man she left her husband for, broke up her family for—someone antisocial and lazy. Now three or so kids have to spend the rest of their childhoods traveling back and forth between two homes. Well, not homes, but rather, houses, two houses. These kids will never have a "home" again because momma had to break up their home to have what this guy had to give her.

I don't blame her. I know what it's like to have excitement and intrigue calling out from behind the walls, and it is dang hard to hold back from the possibility of having a better life than the one you've become bored with. Dang hard.

But, and I'm really talking to myself, we need to keep our heads about the situation.

Let's take antisocial and lazy for example. I'm sure that he was not this way when he caught her eye. He was maybe very social and very anything else that would get her into his bed. Maybe, and maybe it just took a while for his "real person" qualities to appear.

Or maybe not. Maybe it had nothing to do with going to bed. Maybe she also held a key, something she had, something he wanted. Maybe, for example, he desired this married woman because she was very social, and this was something he desperately wanted because maybe he's not very good at talking with strangers.

Then he assumes it is her he wants, when in reality it is her social qualities he desires, not necessarily the woman. He just *thinks* he wants the woman because he can't identify that he really wants her qualities. So then he's got the woman ripped apart from her family. They both got what they thought they needed in each other. And they're with each other. And now, months later, because no one has analyzed, no one has changed, they're both miserable. She's socializing, and he's on the couch.

She doesn't want him. She doesn't know what she wants. And now her family is messed up for good, never to return to the place they once were.

I can tell you what this woman wants. And if we take my theory and run with it, I can figure out very quickly how she's going to get it.

She said, that night at the bon fire, she's looking for the whole package. She wants completion in her man, and because this just isn't reality, because this just isn't out there, what she needs, what she really desires, is completion in herself. I think this is what we all desire, what we all need. We just need to figure out we can get for ourselves what we need and how we can get it apart from a relationship with someone else. Once we have acquired what we need in ourselves, we will then be free in our relationships, no longer expecting someone else to fulfill our desires, dreams, and expectations.

I was pretty snotty to this woman when she first told me her story. I made a hurtful, accusing comment to her. Although it was in laughter, I'm sure the comment came from somewhere not funny. Actually, as soon as I said it, I realized it came from my deepest judgments, and the moment I accused her of "being one of those," an invisible mirror was held to my face. I had already seen and spoken to my fantasy dancer guy a few times by then and suffered a ten-year marriage that I wouldn't have left for anything. This mirror immediately showed me I was accusing her of doing exactly what I had wanted to do for years, but couldn't, and wouldn't.

I no longer judge the family breaker as I judged this woman when I first met her. I thought I was strong. I thought I knew what I was talking about when I committed for better or for worse. I hated my mother for leaving her marriages. I hated my brother-in-law for cheating on my sister. I judged them all as if I was someone so great I could restrain myself from an affair, that I could remain married to the same man forever, no matter what—even with the hurt, rejection, unloving, unsupportive words, and actions. I was committed to my vows no matter what, and I was going to walk this marriage out no matter what. I had no idea what I was sacrificing in myself, or in my children, by doing this.

And I was very successful restraining myself from a sexual affair. But an affair of the heart? That becomes a different story.

My heart, my mind, and my body wanted to be elsewhere. These places cried out from inside of me. They wanted their way. I fought them, trying to keep my vows, but I wasn't winning.

My judgments were going to have their way and prove me wrong. And I was going to walk this road until the end, until my judgments slaughtered me, slaughtered my utopian residency as someone great carrying the queen of restraint banner in the kingdom of marital commitment.

This relationship with fantasy dancer guy was not going to let go of me until I had done everything I ever judged in others. I knew this somewhere deep inside of me. And as much as I wanted the relationship to let me go, I knew I was going to be forced to see this through until I was humbled.

TWENTY

~~~~~~~~~~~

I started thinking after a couple of interesting phone conversations, *why is it we seem to go around dating one kind of man and then end up marrying the complete opposite of that man?* I don't find it coincidental a couple of my friends have done this. And me, this is what I did. And actually, in all three of these relationships, the men we left held very passionate, intimate connections with us, hot, passionate connections. So what was the problem? The problem was they weren't the marrying type.

Did we all just come to a time in our life in which we wanted to be married? Did we trade the deep, passionate, destructive love for a stable and secure one, for a person who would give us our Cinderella ending?

I think I did. And my Cinderella ending has turned into ten years of hushed death.

I didn't want divorce to ever enter my family, no matter what and at all costs. I wasn't going to put my children through the hell I experienced through divorce. This was going to be in my control. And even when, six hours after we were pronounced husband and wife, when he threatened me to walk off the floor during that first dance as husband and wife, I vowed to never let anyone on the outside see how unhappy I was on the inside.

How I wished he had looked at me with eyes filled with adoration and joy, grabbed me, and spun me around out of complete and utter madness of loving this new beginning with his new wife.

But he didn't.

And "they" would never know. Not anyone. Except one did know. I remembered his comment, my neighbor. He said to me one afternoon, as we sat and had a beer together, "You know, you act as if you have the perfect marriage. No one has a perfect marriage."

His comment shocked me, so much so that I didn't have a reply (and rarely do I *not* have a reply).

What did he know that I did not? Of course I have a perfect marriage. I thought I was deceiving the world. I was certainly deceiving myself. I took every betrayal, every hurt, and all dissatisfaction and I tucked them all away very deep—deep inside of myself, not to be viewed by anyone, not even to be viewed by myself. My neighbor wasn't saying anything beyond the fact that no one has a perfect marriage nor should anyone expect to. I should have known this and taken it with a grain of salt. But I couldn't, because I wanted the perfect marriage. His words still ring in my ears when I think of the extent of the imperfection I spent all of my energies hiding.

And so in some sort of half-living I lived, every day until fantasy dancer guy came along and put a magnifying glass on my life.

My great Christian friend (which, by the way, I love her, my nonjudgmental Christian friend, who also realizes everything isn't always as simple as black and white) tells me that I am crossing oceans to other lands. Isn't life like that? We move to many different lands throughout our lives. And the oceans that we ride provide us time to think about, love, and long for that next piece of land in which we will reside for a while. Until it is time to travel again.

My ocean, she begins to describe, is right now, deep, dark, shark infested. "No," I tell her, "my ocean right now is beautiful, bright blue with only creatures of awe, colorful, deep, but clear to the wonderful sandy bottom." My head and my heart are at odds with each other. And that seems to her a miserable place to be in. But for me, revealing the truth, confronting my pain, and finally deciding to do something about that empty water pitcher, is amazingly beautiful.

I'm traveling an ocean in anticipation of the land I'm going to. I'm just not sure which island to choose, the island of logic or the island of longing.

TWENTY ONE

~~~~~~~~~

How will I get over my fantasy dancer guy? When will the day come I have to let him go? Because I *will* have to let him go one day. I am a married woman without the option to leave my marriage.

We were driving back from a great night out with fantasy dancer guy, my therapist-neighbor-friend and I, when she says, "What really is going to be hard is when your friend meets someone, and you have to say good-bye."

I just sat there. I hadn't really thought about it. Did she know more than I did? Why would it bother me to say good-bye? Or why would I even have to say good-bye to my friend?

I felt like crying inside. Maybe I would have let go, and maybe it *would* be hard. But he was just a friend. Wouldn't we just be able to stay friends? I don't want to lose my friend altogether.

He was getting to me. A little. No, not a little, a whole lot. I really enjoyed the conversations we had. He made me laugh. And I adored his laugh. He had this great laugh. He said he doesn't laugh that often which made me a little sad for him. Everyone should laugh. A lot. Every single day. Many times a day. Multiple explosions of laughter daily.

I think maybe that it would be great if my fantasy dancer guy would meet someone—someone great.

Breakups really suck. No matter who they involve, break-ups are really hard.

I'm trying to plan for the day I will say good-bye—the day I will cry.

TWENTY TWO

~~~~~~~~~~

One Sunday I watched this amazing preacher talk about falling to our lustful desires. It was so great I have to get the story in here.

This story was about this guy named Samson. He was an amazing man of amazing strength, blessed by God with an unbelievable gift. The gift was incredible strength in his long flowing uncut hair. God had a purpose for giving this gift of mighty strength to this mighty man. This gift was everything Samson needed to fulfill his destiny in life.

But, we must beware; our greatest strength is rooted directly with our greatest weakness. Our greatest strength *is* our greatest weakness, and our strength is what makes us who we are, so we need it. We just need to know about this connection so we can find the weakness and recognize, confront, and watch for it so it does not, and will not, get in our way, or worse yet, completely destroy us.

If we allow pride to rule our greatest strength, we will fall in complete and utter weakness to that very same strength. This is what happened to this unsuspecting man, Samson.

Samson was a beautiful, desirable man with what would seem to be very large amounts of testosterone to feed those mighty muscles of his. Thus he attracted many desirable women. The very kind, like from that other life, that life far from suburbia married momma life, who take care of themselves. The ones who look so dang good they can cause the lust of a man to rise up from within his deepest most sexual desires.

But these same desirable women were also Samson's enemy.

He knew this, and yet he allowed these beautiful women from enemy territory to draw him to them. He participated in a seven-day bachelor party as he prepared to marry one of these women from enemy territory. A seven-day bachelor party! Dang, and I had issues dealing with the one night! Anyway, Samson gave his fellow celebrating bachelors a riddle to solve by the end of the week. If they figured out the answer, Samson would pay them. They couldn't figure the riddle out, so they went to his wife-to-be and bullied her to find a way to get the answer out of him.

Well, she did what a woman would do to get what she wanted out of a man, she cried whenever the two of them were together. Finally Samson broke and gave her the answer to the riddle. And surprise, surprise, at the celebration, the bachelors had the answer to the riddle and Samson had to pay them.

Samson went about doing his thing, amazing things with his strength. He killed a lion with his bare hands, slaughtered thousands of enemies. He also went about doing his things with his greatest weakness. He picked up women from the enemy territory and slept with prostitutes.

Then he fell in love with Delilah. It's funny, growing up I thought Samson and Delilah was a love story. It's mind blowing to find out it is actually a story of complete destruction out of love, because of love, or maybe not even that. Maybe I should I say lack of love.

Anyway, and I'm telling this in my own words, Delilah, being on the side of the enemy and pressured by her own people to find the source Samson's strength, went to Samson, relying on his weakness. Delilah maybe wore a low cut, cleavage-showing, sexy outfit; sprayed on some spicy perfume; threw her hair back; and asked Samson how those beautiful, mighty muscles got their power. Oh, and by the way, Samson, I need to know because my people want to kill you. Of course she didn't tell him this.

He gave her a phony reply about being tied up with ropes. She tied him up and told him the enemy was coming to get him.

It wasn't the ropes. He busted out of them with his massive, muscle arms and killed the men who came in to kill him.

Samson's lust tempted him when she came to him again, maybe now in some sexy lingerie, and asked again where he got his strength. He responded with another phony reply and once again the enemy couldn't kill him.

You'd think Samson would have played this out in his mind by now. You'd think he might have thought, what would have happened had I told this beautiful woman the truth? But he didn't, or he chose not to, or he just didn't care. Maybe she was too beautiful, and alluring, maybe the chemistry between the two was more powerful than he was.

I think she decided to pull out all the stops and the two were maybe lying in bed naked after a great love-making session, and Samson, upon satisfying his uncontrollable lusty ways, gave her his secret. He had gone over the edge. He crossed the line, never to go back to the moment before, and gave in to his ultimate weakness. He had been warned. Twice. He knew what she was after. He didn't care.

His enemies came in, cut off his beautiful long hair—his God given gift of strength—and gouged his eyes out.

TWENTY THREE

~~~~~~~~~~

It really does hurt to say good-bye. It makes you want to be so much closer to the one you are leaving. Never have I felt so much adoration for this fantasy dancer guy than I did with the thought of saying good-bye. I wanted to tell myself, no, I can't leave, but I have to keep my head and my family together.

I started to believe it was him. I started to believe I wouldn't feel so happy and amazing without him directly in my life. I had gotten myself into such an intense haze I no longer cared who knew about him and me.

I was so extremely happy and alive I wanted to stay that way forever. I knew that I wrote it wasn't about him, but that day I didn't care. Suddenly, I thought, *Oh no.*

I let myself get stuck.

How could I think I was safe, that it was just about sex? How could I think I wouldn't get stuck if I didn't have sex? I was really stupid about this. I let him grip my heart. What was I doing? Better yet, what was I going to do now?

Run. Running is the answer. Run now, while there still is no sex, run, before we have sex.

One of my girlfriends said that when you have this kind of thing going with someone, this pulling, this luring, being in between is the very hardest place to be. You either need to be as far away from this person as you can get, or as close.

Can I get away from him? I don't know. How can I run from him, when all I want to do is run *to* him? I do truly believe that this whole thing is about me, about being me, about coming to life. But how can I now get away from him? How can I keep myself from going so deep into this relationship that I will never crawl out?

TWENTY FOUR

~~~~~~~~~

I was on the phone with my fantasy dancer guy, and I was desperate to find a way to get out of the conversation. His voice was one I began to crave hearing. I was becoming obsessed—with him.

I had to find a way to make him not want to talk to me. At least in the way that he *was* talking to me, trying to drive me insanely mad. I remembered a conversation I had with my great-therapist-neighbor-friend.

She said most of the time these things/relationships will maybe last just a year or two. Yes, like boiling chemistry calming to a simmer. It made sense. Just enough time to realize the fantasy has worn off.

She said when you figure out this person is a real person just like any person, even the person you are with, the thing usually fizzles. I thought about what she said while I was on the phone with him. I didn't want to wait through years of frustrated torment for fantasy dancer guy to see me as a real person, so I told him the worst story about me that I could think of.

I said, "Do you want to see me as a real person?"

He was going to go along with this. He was listening.

I explained how, when I gave birth to my baby girl, for years after I got this irritating, nasty hemorrhoid. Awful and sometimes so painful I would take pain pills to sleep.

Fantasy dancer guy was quiet on the other end of the line. I knew this was going to work. I hated to do it, but I was desperate. I went on with the story about my final frustration of going to see my wonderful doctor whom I adore and I asked him what we could do about it.

He said, "We will cut it out."

Having never gone through something like this, I let him do it. It was the most painful, @#$*ing thing I have ever been through. He held it up for me and said, "My, that's a biggie." I was so impressed myself that I had him jar it up in formaldehyde for me to take home. I showed my massive piece of fleshy whatever-it-was to everyone who visited. (That's real person me—shock value. I can't help it.) Anyway, the story gets worse. Two days later I get another one and had to go for another surgery. The pain was worse. And then another one pops out. My great doctor does another procedure right on top of the others.

I didn't think I could top the first, or the second. Now with three of these surgeries in two days, *this* is the most painful thing I have ever gone through.

My great doctor said, "It's like a can of worms down there." I told him he was very funny and that better be the last worm.

It was.

And so, I finished my gruesome tale and asked my moments-ago-heated, fantasy dancer guy, "So does that make me more of a real person?"

He said, "Yeah."

Sexual temptation was definitely going to be out of the question now. I hung up the phone and laughed out loud. I couldn't believe I did that. But it was great. It was freeing. Everything didn't have to be so mysterious and exciting. And so, as embarrassing as this is, I share this only for the purpose of a really great way for someone trapped in something heavy and intense to quickly turn off the heat. You'll be glad you did. It beats waking up in the morning with an adulterous affair hangover.

I stumbled next door and told my therapist-great-neighbor-friend my story. We laughed hysterically and couldn't stop. I have been told I'm a self saboteur. I guess I am. In this case it was a quality I held necessary and very useful.

TWENTY FIVE

~~~~~~~~~~

A weakness can never be viewed as weak, ever. There is incredible power and strength in weakness.

Weakness has the very power to stifle our lives in its truest form. Like Samson, it keeps us from doing what we need to do, and causes us to do what we should not be doing.

Lust has power in its weakness. It can take over lives, marriages, and homes. Slaughter them, destroy them, and leave them for dead.

Samson's heart, mind, and spirit were given over to lust, a sexual lust so overwhelmingly strong that, in a sense, he let his seducer continue asking, "How do I destroy you? How do I destroy you?" Over and over again.

Delilah was sent into Samson's life to destroy him and he was so blinded by his lust, his greed, and his love for this incredibly sexy woman who made such a major impression on him, he gave her his gift which held everything of value in his life—his strength.

What is your strength? What are you handing over to the enemy when you fall into the trap of weakness and defeat by giving into your lusts? Is it a marriage? Your family? Career? Morals? Values?

The end of Samson was very sad and tragic. He never got the person he was after, the one he had the affair with, the beautiful woman, the one he thought he loved. The one who, maybe after a few nights of hot passionate sex, walked out of his life—**with his life**.

What are we giving over to when we obey those deep crying voices of longing in our hearts and lusting in our bodies? We rarely hear of these carnal liaisons being successful. We rarely hear of someone who walks away whole. No, they walk away injured, maybe with their eyes gouged out, never to be the same again.

Samson lived the rest of his life blinded and with deep sorrow and regret, despair to the very depths of himself. Empty and alone, the gift of God torn from his life forever, he cried out for his own death, and died in his strength-less beauty.

TWENTY SIX

~~~~~~~~~~~~~~~~~~~~~~~~~

My therapist-neighbor-friend did the math for me and it turned out that something like eight people in a hundred leave their families, marry their affair, and make it together.

Eight. In one hundred. The statistics aren't good. And that's only the family breaker. We're not talking about the children and the ex-spouse. I'm sure it's around zero for them—the kids at least. And it's been said that for a child, a divorce marks the end of that child's childhood.

A child after divorce never looks at things in life through the eyes of innocence any more. They never pick up a toad and see it the same, never sit down and have dinner the way they were accustomed to, never get tucked into bed in the same way that mommy and daddy had for so many years. They never wake up on Saturday morning and see daddy cooking breakfast while mommy stands by and drinks coffee.

The end. The end of a childhood of happy innocence.

When you're in a haze, you don't believe any of it. Don't care. You look at those statistics and you see the eight. You think there is possibility within those eight. You think you could be one of those eight. I, too, think positively on that sort of thing. Now if there were zero possibility, I might shrink. But otherwise, I will place myself where I will, and I could place myself with those eight.

It is deception. And if we're not battered, if we're not living in torment, if we're not absolutely miserable in our marriage, then it's probable we won't be in those eight. We should leave if we are living in torment. Leave for the kids. But if we are not, then we should stay. Stay for the kids. I will do everything I can to stay, until I can't stay anymore.

I will be strong. Resist the cravings. When an impulse rises up within me I need to stop and tell myself, this, too, shall pass. And it does pass.

(If I can master this, maybe I can master the quit smoking thing? Yeah, right.)

This fantasy dancer guy thing, I will work through. I will have weak moments, but I will let them pass. I will keep reminding myself that I can take what he gives me with me.

Remind myself my freedom was inside of me, my freedom was always inside of me. Fantasy dancer guy just helped me find the key to unlock the door.

I still go back and forth, and I'm as selfish as a baby trying to give up a bottle. I'm whining and crying inside, not caring about anything else in the world but my bottle. I need to be weaned, like a baby. Sometimes these things take a little time.

And if I can't, in fact, go back to the place I was before, then I am going to be thrilled about that, about being a better person having lived—having lived through my longing for fantasy dancer guy, touching places inside of me that were hidden away forever, bringing things to the surface that needed to be felt, making me realize I was living amongst the walking dead, denying the depths of my pain, and wasting my happiness, wasting my life.

I will never live there again. I am free from the prison within myself. The barred doors have opened and have set my deepest most innermost self free.

And my husband, my kids, I didn't have to set my prison around them to gain my own freedom. It's not about them. It's about me. And I don't want their trust, their security, and their lives to be the payment for my freedom.

TWENTY SEVEN

~~~~~~~~

I am very thankful for the strength God has given me thus far to work through all of this with my fantasy dancer guy. He's not one who has been easy to resist. He is the sweetest dang man I have ever met, one just waiting to give his heart to another who will nurture it.

It seems I can't be that one, and it makes me sad. But I already have many hearts to take care of in my life, and that is something that needs to be done for him by one woman, one very special woman.

I said good-bye to him. I needed to return my attentions fully to seeking my purpose and raising my children. For I love *them* with the greatest love that was ever created.

My heart may be fleeting around right now, but with my children is where my heart is grounded. It is where I belong, where my heart belongs.

They are my people, my most special people in the world, the ones God has entrusted to me, the ones I need to remain with, to love, and to be loved by.

I will never, ever forget him, my fantasy dancer guy.

His amazing laugh is embedded in my heart. I told him that in five years we will be great friends. I hope that happens. I hope when our paths cross one day, he will be telling me of his greatest love, a love who holds all of the things he is looking for, desiring, and wanting for his life.

I hope when I see him again he has a sure, secure home and a grounded, faithful, sexy suburbia-mommy-to-be.

I hope she will be standing by his side, adoring him beyond all other adoration imaginable.

I was prepared for this day, I thought, *the day I would cry.*

I had a dream. I was with fantasy dancer guy and we were in his vehicle. We were in a large mass of water together. My kids may have been there, too. The waters had risen to our necks and the waters felt good. They were cool and crisp and clean. I didn't care about the water. I just looked over and was happy to have my fantasy dancer guy with me.

What I didn't realize in the dream was that the waters were about to go over our heads. I was ready to be drowned in those waters, and I didn't care.

I have to care. I have to realize my feelings of peace and contentment cannot remain. I will drown in this relationship if I don't let go. I have to know I will be sacrificing something so great if I don't let go of him, my fantasy dancer guy.

I know I loved him. I know I can't love him anymore. I have to let him go. I don't want to let him go. I *have* to let him go. Someone once said to me I have to think of myself and my own happiness. But there's a wisdom that says the first shall be last and the last shall be first. No, I cannot think about myself, my happiness. I must think of the others in my life.

Great things come from great sacrifice, and, although I don't know at this point what those great things are, I will believe. And hope. And hold on to this moment of pain which will reap great things for my life and those around me through my act of self-denial.

And so on this day, when I felt the tears well up inside of me, ready to pour forth, I knew it was the day. The day that I would go deep inside of myself to the place that had longed for so many years to be touched and slowly, sadly loosen his grip from my heart.

Good-bye, sweet one. I thank you for the courage you brought to my life. I thank you for the passion you showed me existed in me. I thank you for every good thing you have helped me discover inside of myself. I thank you for making me want to be beautiful, every day. You mean more to me than you will ever know.

Fantasy dancer guy could get me if he tried. He could keep calling out to my heart until I just couldn't bear it anymore. He knows he has the ability to give me what I don't have. He could stand on my island of longing and make himself very beautiful there. Irresistible. Absolutely irresistible with his beautiful self. Alone on that island, just him, calling me. But I know he, too, was letting go.

He told me, "Go. Go and make your marriage work." And with that he also said goodbye.

He cared, too. Cared enough to let me go and point me away from himself. His arm extended, directing me to the logical island on which I belong. The island that is accepted, expected. The island my family and marriage inhabit.

Today is a very bad day. Today I have just existed. My inner music has quieted. I'm dancing a different dance now, one very slow and very sad dance. But with all my heart I know that, this, too, shall pass.

And one day I will once again dance a happy dance.

TWENTY EIGHT

I started thinking about these two islands, the island of logic and the island of longing, and thinking maybe it isn't about who is on these islands. Who resides on each island seems to be some kind of illusion just hovering over these pieces of land. Maybe those islands are a representation of two selves within me. Maybe the ocean that I am traveling now is bringing me to a higher understanding of myself.

The island of logic represents what I am supposed to do, who I am supposed to be, all things expected. Logic represents not stepping beyond boundaries I have created or that have been created for me.

The island of longing is everything possible, what I could be, what I could do, longing for all things unexpected and all things impossible, searching out and finding happiness and freedom.

This is why fantasy dancer guy stands on the island of longing. He represents the possibilities, the unexpected, and the impossible. The island of logic, this is why the husband sits there. He represents what is expected of me.

The islands are not about them, nor are they about choosing between them. The islands are about me.

I feel like I have spent many years of this ten-year marriage living in marital death. The man I have lived with has never loved me for me. Has never stood by and cheered my highest accomplishments in life, and he sure hasn't hushed about my greatest defeats. Looking away from fantasy dancer guy and toward my husband is killing me. Allowing him to win is completely heartbreaking, and, worse yet, I can't stop myself from wanting to see my fantasy dancer guy. But it's not either of them. Even when I say that, I know it's not them. It's what they stand for in *my life*. It's not the difference between the husband and the fantasy dancer guy. It's the difference between looking at pain and looking at possibility.

And I need to figure out whether I can go back to that pain and that emptiness. Am I called to live my next ten years exactly as I have lived my last?

My perfect marriage facade has been ripped from me. Everyone knows now. Now I have been set free. How can I go back? Why would I want to?

TWENTY NINE

~~~~~~~~~~

I'm still traveling my ocean, in anticipation, to the land that I may set my feet upon. Both men have faded from the islands; both men have faded from my life, at least partially. Now I stand alone looking at two pieces of land.

One is filled with sadness and defeat. One is filled with possibility and hope. I have resided on that land of sadness, the land of the expected. There were hurricanes there that scared the hell out of me and tribal warriors there who defeated me. I can't seem to bring myself to look back at that logical island.

But I still believe it isn't about fantasy dancer guy, nor is it about being with the other person in anyone's extramarital affair, with sex or without. And even when I have doubted, and started to think it may be the fantasy dancer guy I want, that I may have to trash this whole book and theory, God reveals more truth. And the theory stands strong. It just doesn't end the way I thought it would, or the way I would have liked it to end.

Anyway, it may be that I can't walk away from my relationship with fantasy dancer guy and just take a piece of what he has given me and walk right back into the life I've lived for ten years. For somehow in this whole experience, I have changed. I have felt freedom from my self-imposed prison. Fantasy dancer guy has become more than just a mirror; he has become an escape door for me.

I try to convince myself that fantasy dancer guy is just a guy like my husband, like many husbands, one who is capable of making mistakes, betraying a wife, blowing off a decade of marriage, saying hurtful things. A clean slate does look appealing, but the fact is that the slate will not remain clean. For me, it is not about a clean slate.

For me, it's about falling madly and passionately in love with another man. One I can't seem to find the strength to stay away from. One I didn't walk away, or run away, from soon enough.

Ten years I settled for being number two in my husband's life. His family told me this many times. Their words echoed in my ears, "Hunting and fishing are his first love, you will be second." And somehow, because the mother and grandmother lived their lives this way with their husbands, I, too, assumed I was to accept this and live my life being number two.

It was thrown matter-of-fact into my face many times. And it killed me. It made me feel unimportant. And bitterness infested me.

My husband admits he took for granted I would always be there, admits he spent many years of our marriage with little care and concern for me. He tells me he didn't care about a decade of marriage and the ring I asked for. He didn't have time to get this anniversary gift. He didn't have time to plan, order, and give me a representation of what a decade of my life with him was worth to him.

I stood by him, forgiving his stabs and betrayals. I survived the struggle of raising his babies as he carried on with his freedom many weekends every hunting and fishing season. He had ten years. And ten years wasn't enough, wasn't enough anything. It makes me cry to the depths of my soul, and I feel injured beyond repair. And now he finally wants to care because someone else came along and cared, about something, about me.

THIRTY

~~~~~~~~~~

I spoke with my dad today. My dad tells me I am doing to my husband exactly what my mother did to him. I'm thinking *this can't be true. It's not the same.* I hate my mother for the type of life she lived, leaving him and raising her kids in separate houses. It just wasn't the same. I had a long list of justifiable reasons to leave my husband and go after true passion in my life. Didn't I?

I asked him how long they were married. I'm thinking it was only a few years, not long enough to really know each other. He told me nine years.

When I got off the phone, I started thinking.

She left with a crazy wild guy after nine years. I hated her for it and judged her for it. And now I was doing the exact same thing with *this* wild fantasy guy, to my husband, and to *my* kids.

My mother's second marriage lasted about five years. It started with maybe visions of heaven and ended with burns from the pits of hell.

And she loved that crazy guy. She loved her crazy guy with so much passion that she left almost a decade of marriage and a safe, secure love to be with him. My mother left a man who would have taken care of her forever. And leaving that first marriage may be her biggest regret in life.

When was it I decided I wanted, once again, that passionate, destructive love in place of a secure, safe one? It could have been the day I decided I never felt freer or more like myself than when I was with this other man. But being "more like myself" was who I always was, not who I'd become.

I spent the last ten years becoming someone else, someone I didn't like, someone I didn't like being. I was really stuck, stuck being a wife and a mommy and that's all. Anytime I stepped out to pursue a passion, my husband ridiculed it and hated me for it.

The women in his life were nothing more than wife, mommy, housekeepers—all of them. Not one woman in his life has ever stepped past the boundaries of being wife and mother. He didn't understand me. He didn't understand why I wanted to be more, why I *needed* to be more.

So if I left my husband, ran off with my crazy fantasy dancer guy, and lived in this passionate, destructive state of love, what will that mean? What are the implications of such a love?

I've said fantasy dancer guy could do anything or be anything and I wouldn't care (the A list thing). And when I thought about this, I realized this is an extremely dangerous sort of love. This man could do anything. Think about this, when I say anything, I mean *anything*—at least for a while— maybe a long while.

If I were to wrap myself up with him, how far would I go? How far would I let him go with my life? And everyone involved in my life? What would my life be if I left my husband for any fantasy dancer guy type?

My biggest fear, my heaviest judgment, and my deepest hatred has come up to bite me in my rear. I was never, ever going to be like my mother. And now, I *am* her, and I'm walking *her* steps on a path I hated, a path I swore I would never travel. I'm following her, almost exactly.

I see the picture very clearly now. I'm just not sure if I can control it. Or stop it. My mother, the mirror. How do I break the mirror?

Maybe I am just destined to make my mother's mistakes. Maybe I just can't control my feelings now. What if my fantasy dancer guy is better than hers? Could I convince myself of this and just walk away from my marriage? Take my chances and have this possibly end up being my biggest regret in life? What if I walk away from fantasy dancer guy and live in the same miserable crap? And what if I don't, what if I think I'll be happier with my fantasy dancer guy?

THIRTY ONE

~~~~~~~~~~

The day is here again. The day we plan to say good-bye. We've broken up before and this is going to be our third attempt to break off our intense friendship. We met at a spot we've been before. We had an amazing time together the last time we were here, so amazing it convinced me I really wanted to be with him.

I had this sense all along that my time with this beautiful man was limited, but I refused to think about it whenever I was with him. I would just be with him in the moment, savoring every second my eyes could at least consider him. *Could I make him mine? Should I make him mine? And if I make him mine, would I always be this happy? Or would I look back and hate myself for doing exactly what I despised?*

This moment wasn't like those moments. It wasn't a considering day. This day really had no possibilities or potential.

We stay distant for a while. I don't think either one of us wants this to happen. But it has to happen. Again. And we talk about why it has to happen. We joke about the fact that maybe we should have just had the sex and our connection wouldn't have gone so far. But that was a joke. We really don't want to cheat, not that way. Or maybe we want to and something, or someone, just keeps us from that. Maybe this book.

This day held one last kiss. This moment held one last time to feel his arms around me. This was the one last time I would lay my head on his shoulder. My eyes saw one last smile; my ears heard one last laugh.

I wanted to be strong. I wanted to take this, let the attraction be what it is, and walk away stronger, better, braver, freer. I want to walk away with what this sweet man gave me. The gifts, the memories, the eye opening act of revealing what I was feeling about my empty life and about my deceptive marriage.

I wanted to be strong, but I was far, far, from being strong.

THIRTY TWO

~~~~~~~

I sit in my car, watch him leave, pull away from our spot, and he's gone. I sit up in my seat and start my car. I feel pain rising up inside of me. As a matter of fact, I feel deep in my heart the pain of almost every single boyfriend breakup I experienced in my life.

Every man I really loved and walked away from still in love, I see them one by one. I visualize their faces. I hear their names. There are sad echoes in my heart. They are all still there. Every one gathered in one place inside of me. And it hurt. Deeply.

I'm going home, but I'm not quite ready to just go on with life as usual. I have a score to settle, maybe with myself. I find myself moments later sitting outside on the deck of a little bar overlooking a calm, settled body of water, and I am all alone on this sweet little deck with my own little waitress and an attached bar full of liquor.

The day is perfect. The sky is blue with scattered soft white clouds, the sun shining, the ducks sunning themselves in the water, the birds playing with each other over the lake.

All is well with the world, and the day? Perfect. My life? Not even close. I feel very far away from this immense blessing I'm beholding in the atmosphere.

I lift my glass of straight-up Jack and pour it down my throat. I hold back tears that were screaming to get out. I am strong and independent. I need no man, not one who doesn't appreciate me, and not the crazy one I desired, either. How has my happy, beautiful life gone into such turmoil? Mere weeks is all it took to go from a sleeping housewife to a fully alive passionate human, only to be deathly saddened by such loss in my life as this amazing man walks out.

I order another Jack and look over the lake, trying to convince myself God did not create the waters for us to drown ourselves in. I ponder how the very things which give us life also bring death if we misuse them.

I can't let myself believe this is the case with my fantasy dancer guy. It can't be, can it? This is not the job of our prince, to bring harm. At least that is not what I was taught by every love story that ever existed. This wasn't how these things were supposed to end.

But this *is* how it was ending. *This* love story. Just ending. What really was this Cinderella fantasy that made me think it could all end with happily ever after?

I am really starting to get bitter in my thoughts. I feel the sadness turning to anger, very quickly. It's just not fair; it's just not right. Happily ever after?

@#$% Cinderella, @#$% Snow White, @$#% the seven dwarfs, I hate them all! I want to kick her a—, this Cinderella! I'm going to go to Florida, and I'm going to kick her @#$%ing a—! And then, I am going to burn down her castle. Burn it down and spit on the ashes.

I throw another shot of Jack down my throat, look out at that lake and call my fantasy dancer guy. He is impressed. (I love that laugh.) He laughs, "You made it a whole thirty minutes."

Thirty minutes and three shots of Jack, this *is* very impressive if I say so myself. He let me vent, and I carried on my story.

"...and that white horse? I'm going to rip his balls off and shoot him in the head! And then I will sue Disney for being such @#$%-ups with their bull@#$% stories of happily ever after."

Why do we torture ourselves with this crap? Why do we open our minds and hearts to garbage that just doesn't exist? Ever. Why are we so against the truth and why would we hate to get to the end of the story and read,

Cinderella and her prince? Oh yeah, *never*, ever to live happily ever after—

—because it doesn't @#$%ing exist, stupid #$%!

What's so wrong with that? At least we won't get our hopes up. Maybe then there would be fewer people hammered off of straight shots of Jack after the breakup.

THRITY THREE

~~~~~~~~

The thing is Cinderella should have just stayed in her ashes for a while. She should never have had to search for the other half of herself, outside of herself.

She should not teach a gazillion little girls that they need to search for the other half of themselves outside of themselves. She had her prince, or should I say what she needed from her prince, with her, in her, even in the fire pit.

But maybe she got it together before she went and searched out her prince. It is possible, I guess. We never really saw this, her hammering out her life and accepting herself for who she was. But maybe this happened somewhere in her pain of scrubbing the floors and whatever other slave work she was doing.

It would be nice if she had informed us of her amazing self revelations if it did happen while she drudged over a wash bin of dirty water.

And Snow White. When was her big revelation? When she slept for however many years she slept? Did she just dream this? I thought for a minute, maybe I'm messed up. Maybe the fairy tale has these components.

No, no, no. They were all miserable in their circumstances and sought out the prince to whisk them away from their miserable lives. This is a bunch of crap. No flesh man is going to ride up on a white horse, suddenly make you whole, and ride you off into the sunset to live happily ever after.

Our wholeness, our completeness comes from within, and only from within, without our human prince.

THIRTY FOUR

~~~~~~~~~~~~~~~~~~~~~~~~~

I've decided to break away from both my husband and fantasy dancer guy for a little while. Now they are both gone, and I can make the decision myself without blurred man-faces over my islands.

I'm going to throw out an anchor for a while and see what happens, float around in this beautiful, clear, crisp ocean water. Maybe kick back in my boat, get a nice, tropical tan while I vacation from such major life decisions.

Being alone doesn't sound all that bad. It may not be this way for everyone, but everyone planning to leave a marriage should really plan on being alone—for a very long time. For this is the highest possibility or maybe the worst.

And sometimes we should plan for the worst and follow our path to the worst possible outcome. Will our decision be the same?

Maybe the path with the safest outcome is the one we should choose. If not, we can begin to plan for a very hard journey.

At least one thing remains the same as I go through this book, the one thing I want to remain the same, the non-affair, not cheating on my husband. I expected in the beginning to go back to my marriage. Now I'm not as sure. I guess I have even another lesson in that. That affair, while it does point to something lacking within us, it also reveals something lacks within the marriage. Something's missing in our marriage.

I think the honesty I held with my husband through this whole thing will be key in what happens from here. If I snuck around with a sexual affair, it would have ended in just one of three ways.

I could have what I need for the moment, and never reveal anything to him and then walk back into the same situational marriage. Or, if he discovered the affair, our marriage would just end in angry divorce, or more years of hurt and contempt between us if we stayed together.

Truth is important to me and the thing is I didn't look for an affair. The fact this thing is in my face eventually told me, told us, there is something very wrong with our marriage.

We search ourselves. And we search our marriages. We heal ourselves, *because we can*. We heal our marriages, *if we can*.

THRITY FIVE

~~~~~~~~~~~~~~~~~~

Because of my fantasy dancer guy, my journey, wherever it carries me, brings peace and release, contentment and joy, freedom and hope. I no longer sit in judgment about the people and their situations around me. I become afraid every time I feel judgment come. I stop myself and I think, *don't even go there, it could happen to you!* Somewhere along the line it became more imperative for me as a human being to lose my judgments, even if it meant I would lose my marriage in the process.

Thanks to my fantasy dancer guy, I'm not watching movies with a wall up. I'm not listening to music with a wall. I no longer read with a wall or write with one.

I dance inside, a dance of possibility and a future. I know *this* dance will not last forever. There are always dances of sadness mixed with dances of joy. But I haven't danced for a long time. I haven't heard any music in which to dance to for a very long time. And sometimes, aren't even slow, sad dances better than no dance at all?

The ring on the phone surprised me. I wasn't expecting a call. The voice on the other line brought the same reaction it did the very first time I heard its memory of that very first night echoed inside my head—my bones melted, my heart pounded, and fire surged through me. Our time apart, our attempted breakups, and my final decision to let my marriage go, brought my fantasy dancer guy back to me. It seems he, too, found himself unable to let go.

~~~~~~~~~~~~~~~~~~~~

I have fallen in love with a man,
One from whom I should have fled,
But couldn't.

~~~~~~~~~~~~~~~~~~~~

SOME FINAL THOUGHTS FOR YOUR RELATIONSHIP

~~~~~~~~~

What propels a marriage to fail? When does it become so torturous we decide we can't live in our state of sanctimonious union any longer? How far have we really gone when we are willing to sacrifice our families, our homes, our assets? Is a relationship salvageable in its seeming destruction, or have we crossed over to the point of no return?

Fantasy dancer guy admires the roses on our table. The glass vase filled with red, bright green, and touches of small white dots brightened the room for five days. The red petals stand strong in their vibrant glory. "Those roses have lasted quite a long time," is his simple comment. Then he adds, "You know what they say about fast dying roses?"

I thought for just a moment. "Fast dying love?" I guess.

"Yeah," he answers. I smile.

I took quite some care with these roses. When I received them I carefully immersed the stems in a cold bath and trimmed the bottoms to a forty-five degree angle, then did it again after a couple of days. A couple days after that I considered using a procedure to bring back life to the one stem that was becoming weak. I filled my whole tub with cold water and let the flower bathe for a while.

I pondered my care and concern for that one flower amidst its eleven others and my fantasy dancer guy's words echo in my mind, *fast dying roses, fast dying love*. Of course. If I were to throw those roses in a vase and forget about them, they may last two or three days. They'd look terrible in a week with dry, crusted edges, weak necks on all twelve, petals falling around their clear, glass stand. Neglect of my roses equals fast dying roses. And neglect of my love equals fast dying love.

To nurture is the opposite of neglect. If I nurture my roses I produce the opposite result that neglect produces. The opposite of dying is living. If I nurture my roses I will sustain a living organism, but this is impossible to happen without my personal care. A living organism cannot remain a living organism unless I help it live under my care and concern for its life.

Everything around us is a result of nurture or neglect, some in our control, some outside of it.

The grass, neglected of rain, will wither and die. On the other hand, the grass, watered by the heavens weekly, will prosper, grow, and have life.

A house neglected will eventually produce a leaky roof, which in turn, continued neglect will cause all of its contents to rot and be destroyed. A home nurtured will be warm and cozy, its contents safe and protected from the cold winds and rain.

Neglect will cause something to become very unappealing—to the eye, to the senses. If I neglect my roses, they will quickly die and only be suitable for the garbage can.

Neglect causes loss.

Neglect your homework and you will lose your high grade. Neglect your job? You will lose your job. Neglect your electricity bill, your phone bill? You will lose your power and your telephone. Neglect your car and eventually it will run no longer.

Neglect your spouse? Then eventually you will lose your spouse.

I spoke with a friend about his marriage trouble. He's worried his wife won't be around forever. He wants to be assured of her presence in their marriage five, ten years from now, and if he doesn't have that assurance from her right now, he sees no reason to keep the marriage together.

He misses the point. He wants a guarantee for the future when the only real guarantee is the moment we are in right at this point. Who knows what will be a minute from now, let alone ten years! But there is a secret. There is a way. One that works just with the speculation that there will be a future, a minute from now, or ten years.

Nurture is the answer. Without nurture you will make a thing suitable only for the garbage, only to end up in the dump, no longer pleasing to look at, to live around.

My friend should not fret about the future, he should **do what he can in the moment to ensure the result he *wants* for the future.** If he wants his wife to stay devoted to their marriage, then he should do everything he can to give her no reason to *leave* the marriage! If she is loved, if she is cared for, if she is nurtured, she will go nowhere!

IN CONCLUSION:

Tiffany Twisted & Some Dance: What my books have taught me

~~~~~~~~~

Judgment, whether swift or devised, usually results in pain on the side of the receiver. When we judge, we put ourselves in a place of authority that says, "I know what is good for you, I know what is right for your life." Think of things you might have judged throughout your life. Can you find something you thought wrong a time ago and now have changed your point of view? What happened between then and now? More than likely you have grown, matured. Maturity and growth have wrought a different point of view.

It's as simple as my distaste for onions when I was young. If there were onions on something I would make sure I would give it a long, *eeewwww*, regardless of where I was or who created the dish. Imagine a buffet line at a birthday party, reunion, or church potluck. I'm walking through and I come across a dish that looks interesting, I pick up the spoon and toss it around in the dish a little bit contemplating the ingredients. I see an onion and I give it a long, *eeewwww*, and pass on the dish.

Now maybe the person who spent hours in the kitchen making this dish was behind me. She sees and feels my rejection. She doesn't understand my distaste for the onion, she took it as a rejection to the whole package. Now I have grown and matured to like onions and put them on almost anything, but in my ignorance to voice my personal opinion, I have hurt people along the way.

That is a small example, but should speak volumes to the person who is open to searching themselves out. This is the first step to doing away with our judgments—be prepared to look at yourself and your motives.

Anytime we look at the outside of something and draw a conclusion without fully understanding, we are in judgment. This is why judgment can only be the job of God. He is the only one who fully understands. We have no right to judge a person or a situation based on a conclusion from what we see or perceive.

My conservative friend stood before my creative daughter, taking in her bright pink hair and a lip ring. Ugly and unattractive were the words she used. Her judgment was about the outside, what she saw. It was not her taste, and she expressed her "eeeeewwwww." And as a result, she rejected the whole package. When my daughter thinks about herself, will she feel this character defeating "eeewwww" from this woman?

Why was the conversation focused only on the outside, only on what this grown woman deemed inappropriate? Why couldn't she have spoken about my daughter's straight A grades in school, or what she was wearing to the homecoming dance next week?

Judgment can be very painful to the person receiving it, and whether we mean well trying to save someone from the pits of hell, or just from embarrassing themselves, we need to always do everything out of love.

Ask yourself, am I presenting this judgment out of love, or am I presenting it out of some kind of superior knowledge or pride? Am I going to help this person, or cause this person pain? If you are presenting your judgment to raise your own self in pride, you have made yourself the enemy. When you can honestly say you are speaking out of love and not for injury, you have made yourself a friend. Freedom from judging, as well as freedom from judgment, is freedom defined.

A LETTER TO MY MOM

~~~~~~~~~~~

Dearest Mummy,

I said in my first book, TIFFANY TWISTED, *I despised you. And now, here, in this book, I became you. And I believe I walked your steps, so that I, in the end, could understand you.*

I know it is hard for you to read what I write, but I do hope you get here. I need to confess my wrongs against you. I need to tell you how sorry I am for every judgment I held against you. I need your forgiveness. Desperately. And, although, I do know you will forgive me freely, I need to say more.

I am sorry for standing before you as if I knew so much. I don't know so much. And just as easily as you, I was torn away. And just as easily as you, I could make mistakes you made. And I hate myself for hating you. I never hated you. I love you. I love you as much as any daughter could love her mother.

You are a wonderful mummy. And thank you for everything I never thanked you for. I really, really don't know how you did as well as you did. I mean that from the bottom of my heart.

And please, be well, and okay with everything. Nothing happens without God's consent. Our lives, how they happen, are his will. Be at peace, my dearest mummy. It is all worked for the good. Your loving daughter, TT

ABOUT THE AUTHOR

~~~~~~~~~~

Tiffany Twist is the author of *TIFFANY TWISTED: exposed, unraveled, rewritten,* (June 2004 by et al. Publishing ISBN: 1931945179) and *SOME DANCE: Hey bartender, I'll take a decade of marriage on the rocks, a therapist straight up, and a fantasy guy with a twist* (2005 by et al. Publishing ISBN: 1931945306) She is also a business owner, screenwriter, and mother to four. Tiffany resides in Minnesota with her family. Visit her web site at www.tiffanytwist.com.